Douglas Dunn was born in 1942 and grew up in Inchinnan in Renfrewshire. He worked as a librarian in Britain and the United States until 1971, when he became a full-time writer. His sixth collection of poems, *Elegies*, was Whitbread Book of the Year for 1985. He has also won the Somerset Maugham Award, the Geoffrey Faber Memorial Prize, the Hawthornden Prize and the Cholmondeley Award. In 1991 he was appointed Professor in the School of English at the University of St Andrews.

The Year's Afternoon

DOUGLAS DUNN

faber and faber
LONDON·NEW YORK

First published in 2000
by Faber and Faber Limited
3 Queen Square London WC1N 3AU
Published in the United States by Faber and Faber, Inc.,
an affiliate of Farrar, Straus and Giroux, New York

Photoset by Wilmaset Ltd, Wirral
Printed in England by MPG Books Ltd,
Victoria Square, Bodmin, Cornwall

A CIP record for this book
is available from the British Library

ACKNOWLEDGEMENTS
Some of the poems in this collection first appeared in *The Formalist,
The Herald, Modern Painters, New Scottish Writing*(Soho Square, no. 7),
*The North, Poetry Ireland, Poetry Review, Prism, The Red Wheelbarrow,
TLS, Verse* and *West Highland Free Press*

ISBN 0-571-20427-9

2 4 6 8 10 9 7 5 3 1

In Memoriam
SJB and GBJ

Contents

The Year's Afternoon 3
A European Dream 6
Pre- 9
A Theory of Literary Criticism 11
T. E. Lawrence at The Ozone 12
Song 14
Scott's Arks 15
Parrot Islands 17
'Contemporary Scottish Writing' 18
Agates 19
1996 20
Sunrise 21
Art is Wonderful 22
Teachers 26
A Complete Stranger 30
Three Poets 32
The Black Douglas 37
Woodnotes 38
Leopardi 41
Pushkin's Ring 44
If Only 47
On Whether Loneliness Ever Has a Beginning 48
March 13, 1994 57
You 58
Native Meditation 59
Night Watch 60
Dinner 61
Out of Breath 62
Venezuela 65
The Wasp House 66

East Riding 67
Bête Noire's Edition of *Terry Street*
   with Photographs by Robert Whitaker 69
Martagon Lilies 73
Early Hours in Dairsie 77
Indolence 79

The Year's Afternoon

The Year's Afternoon

As the moment of leisure grows deeper
I feel myself sink like a slow root
Into the herbaceous lordship of my place.
This is my time, my possessive, opulent
Freedom in free-fall from salaried routines,
Intrusions, the boundaryless tedium.
This is my liberty among trees and grass
When silence is the mind's imperfect ore
And a thought turns and dallies in its space
Unhindered by desire or transactions.
For three hours without history or thirst
Time is my own unpurchased and intimate
Republic of the cool wind and blue sea.
For three hours I shall be my own tutor
In the coastal hedge-school of grass furniture.
Imaginary books fly to my hand
From library trees. They are all I need.
Birdsong is a chirp of meditative silence
Rendered in fluttered boughs, and I am still,
Very still, in philosophical light.
I am all ears in my waterside aviary.
My breath is poised for truth to whisper from
Inner invisibilities and the holiness
Venturesome little birds live with always
In their instinctive comforts. I am shedding
The appetites of small poetry and open to
Whatever visits me. I am all eyes
When light moves on water and the leaves shake.
I am very still, a hedge-hidden sniper
In whose sights clarified infinity sits

[3]

Smiling at me, and my skin is alive
To thousands of brushed touches, very light
Delicate kisses of time, thought kisses,
Touches which have come out of hiding shyly
Then go back again into the far away
Surrender they came from and where they live.
Perfecting my afternoon, I am alert to
Archival fragrances that float to me
Unexplained over the world's distances.
This is my time. I am making it real.
I am getting rid of myself. This is my time.
I am free to do whatever I wish
In these hours, and I have chosen this
Liberty, which is an evanishment
To the edges of breath, a momentary
Loss of the dutiful, a destitute
Perchance, a slipping away from life's
Indignities and works into my freedom
Which is beyond all others and is me.
I am free to do as I like, and do this;
I sink like a slow root in the name of life
And in the name of what it is I do.
These are my hours of 1993.
Ears, eyes, nose, skin and taste have gone.
For a little while I shall be nothing and good.
Then other time will come back, and history.
I shall get up and leave my hiding place,
My instinctive, field-sized republic.
I shall go home, and be that other man.
I shall go to my office. I shall live
Another year longing for my hours
In the complete afternoon of sun and salt.

My empty shoes at the bedside will say to me,
'When are we taking you back? Why be patient?
You have much more, so much more, to lose.'

A European Dream

I dreamt I missed the bus from Łomza down to Warsaw.
It was raining, a rain that varnished skin and clothes.
I wandered past the turn for Ostrałenka, preferring
Views of thin horses in pastures by stagnant roadsides
To thumbable cars and big trucks from Gdynia and Gdansk.
Policemen, farmers, and postmen with airmails passed me;
They paid me no attention, in my thornproof Border tweeds,
My briefcase and umbrella, as my Scottish brogues
Leathered the tarmac, a credit to Hoggs of Fife.
They might have thought me just another journalist
Pedestrian factfinding in industrial Ruritania
Instead of someone dreaming what almost happened.
Words in my mouth, as I talked to myself, were strangers
To each other. Crossroads' traffic, changing gear in Polish,
Was language of great charm and great Copernicus,
Spoken Chopin, the passion of Slavonic eloquence.
Night fell with cushioned landings on the active forests.
Wooded nocturnes made me feel that the continent
Widened across humanity's north-European plain
As tops of conifers twinkled in the starlight
With epic whisperings that said 'Pan Tadeusz, Pan Tadeusz'.
Wolf, bear and bison staggered from the dens of species,
Hunted down, parked, tamed, zoo'd, or modernized,
Turned into jerkins or the privileged plateful.
Time, too, was walking in the night, counting the graves,
Re-paragraphing chronicles of howls and tears.
I heard a river wash its scraps of sunken armour.
Sword-shards, helmets, crankshafts, to a listening ear
Sounded as sub-aqueous and subterranean nudges
On skulls and bones and residue of hoof and steel,

Eyes and flesh, the pure substance of massed memories, melted
Into historical compost. I dreamt the darkest night
I ever knew and time was strolling beside me
Down that road at the hour of no cars and no one. Time
Felt disinclined to lend a hand and help me through.
'Feel hard and think historical' – I left the road
Out of obedience to my sturdy aphorism
With golf umbrella up and a firmly gripped briefcase
And through long, lighted windows I saw kissing of hands
At a big do beneath archaic chandeliers
As chauffeurs polished limousines by candlelight,
Their little vodkas balanced on their polished cars.
For several surreal moments I was at the soirée
Kissing the hand of this one, that one, being diplomatic,
Temporarily suave in black tie and dinner jacket
Or just as out-of-place in Border tweed (three piece)
Among the ball-gowned and Old European tuxedo'd
Counts and Margraves, leaders, luminaries, a cardinal,
A consumptive poet, generals, celebrated courtesans,
Which is to say too little of East Prussians,
Muscovian footpads, Lithuanians and leather Scots
Pedlars and mercenaries, Swedes, Red Cavalrymen,
Ubiquitous Italian waiters and Parisian chefs
Voluble with genius and pedigree'd certification,
Greatcoated Tartar grooms and Cossack major-domos.
Then I was fighting off the tugs and rips of briars
In multiplying forests, or watching my wife
Led one way and my children the other, myself that way,
At the dummy station among the tight-leashed dogs
In the stench of cattle-truck excrement, with glimpsed timetables
Listing departures for Vienna, and *that* city, and *that* town,

And the grin of the officer with his hands on his hips.
Bon voyage! I shouted, as I ran through the forest
In the endless night, very deep with timber inwit,
Running like a tormented innocent through slumber
Twisted by European odiousness and what happened
In that neck of the woods. *Bon voyage!* I cried again
To myself and the millions as I ran on,
Umbrella ripped from my hand and my briefcase dropped
Into a gurgling drainage ditch, my 'life's work'
Bundled down to its watery rot where croaking toads live
And my suit made by Stewart and Christie of Edinburgh
Ripped into the rags of one hungering for want, torn by
Hunger for hunger and a loud curse on all comfort,
Hunger for lyrical anger, for righteous indignation,
Vituperative and lonely in the forests of hopelessness.
I woke up as a man beaten, scratched and filthy
In the torn clothes of an interior adventure
Shouting, 'Shrive me more for what I haven't committed!
Negate even my soul if I have one as I plead before
The pagan God of Kindness who doesn't exist!'
History's wide-boys and murderers tittered and giggled,
Experts in *mauvaise foi*, forgetfulness, and shameless
Persistence in their arts of perpetuity and success.
'Goodbye,' I said to myself, parting company with
My own certainties, my body, my name, my language.
It is disagreeable, to tend your garden, on your knees,
With the sensation of tending millions of graves.

Pre-

It goes back to a time when stones were new
And there was no one to wonder at the sun
Rising above the rims of everything.

It is the dawn's visible echo tells me
That before philosophies of me and you
There was unpopulated wilderness and such

Absent desire the mind can't think of it
For there was neither mind nor name nor us
In that pre-onomastic clocklessness.

Molecular events began in fishless seas.
All-continental silence held its hush
As of all the breaths of the future being held

And stone was waiting (as it were) insensibly,
Precious, and semi-precious, ignorant of time
Before the cults of measurement and value.

Creation was inching its way through millennia
Towards the invention of flesh and ethics.
Coal, diamonds, gold, were being made beneath

Surfaces, in the insensate factories.
There were storms in the ground, and blazing stones,
And no one knows what colour was the sky.

Involuntary, microscopic steps
Led to our moment, the birth of the first time
On a pre-religious planet without eyes.

In all that mish-mash of invention, love
Occurred, in chemistry, in man and woman,
In stone, in fire, in animals, and me, and you.

And if there was no Garden, no Paradise –
The leafy bield, the flowers, the gentle creatures,
Abundance and no shame, love, and no thorns –

The story is too good for disbelief, too true,
The first of poems and first of tragedies,
The invention of death, and love, and error.

A Theory of Literary Criticism

In 1930, on the island of Java,
Pablo Neruda purchased Shakespeare's *Sonnets*
Into which he wrote his name and the date.

After he died, his houses were plundered.
What became of his book, his treasure of four decades?
Whether stolen, or cast aside, it circulates

From Batavia to Chile by the long way round
Across the Indian Ocean and the South Atlantic,
From Chile to Batavia across the Pacific.

It goes like an albatross and they cannot kill it.
Out of the fires of burning books rises the perfect replica.
From hand to phantasmagorical hand

It visits 'the perfume of pomegranates in Verona',
'The vulgar voices of parasites and buffoons',
And touches men and women to the quicks of their lives.

Burning purifies it. They cannot kill it.
It runs off the printing presses; and they cannot kill it.
They discuss it in lecture theatres but cannot kill it.

Were it sought out by police everywhere, and none remained,
Keepers of verse would whisper it to others
And teach them with memory's astounding patience.

They would write it down for them, in every language.
Anything made can be unmade, but with this exception –
If it exists, it exists, and there is the chance of eternity.

T. E. Lawrence at The Ozone

in memoriam George Kendrick

If Bridlington appears the sort of place
No one of consequence would linger in
Beyond the close of business, it's not true.
Here T. E. Lawrence messed about in boats
And, once demobbed, was put up at The Ozone.
What this has to do with you, George, old friend,
Might be just one of those mysteries of verse
We used to talk about. It's Bridlington,
Of course it is, and Lawrence's lost Ozone,
As well as where you were born, a place you liked,
And I liked too, on that day together,
Drinking beer, eating fish, listening to
Your anecdotes of Suez, teaching, verse,
As you unwinded, and we talked about
T. E. Lawrence and the vanished hotel.
No longer in the *Yellow Pages*, gone
Into the guest-house annals, second-hand
Emporia where knapery and cutlery
Circulate among passed-on furniture, plates,
Cups and saucers, I think about Lawrence
In a lost room at the end of his service
On his last days here, writing his letters,
Preparing for ununiformed existence,
A few years more to polish his enigma.
Down at the harbour, through a smell of fish,
A scent gets through, distilled in Araby,
Sandalwood, coffee, frankincense and myrrh,
And someone senior to him saying 'Sir'
Split seconds after he had slipped away

Into the ether in his demob suit
Heading to destiny from destiny
On his Homeric motorcycle.
Dear George, my memory of you, somehow
Or other (such *is* the mystery) is here,
Too – Bridlington harbour, talk, fish, and beer
Remembered in a sensation of *always*
And shared *Gauloises*, walking along the pier
Speaking of life and poetry, the ways
In which a line or two can say so much
Existence. Old friends being philosophical!

Song

All day I've thought of a bird's bones
Discovered in grass at a pavement's edge
On my walk in the lunch hour,
Its small, thin, delicate skull
Weightless in my cupped hand,
And I'll preserve it
Until I forget.
As light as a finch's eye carried
On the twigs of its legs and feet
Towards Creation's funeral,
My inmost bird, my chance of song,
Goes with me and within me,
As light as the smoke from my cigarette.

Scott's Arks

Over her laundry, suds, scrubbing board, tub,
A girl in service wiped her brow and saw
Windowed *Discovery* in the steam's wet thaw,
Its haze and cloudy drips. Imperial hub

For a moment – the jute about to go –
Dundee and Tay filled an ancestral lung
To cheer the heroes and sing for a far-flung
Imperial classless continent of snow.

Frostbitten fingers died before the heart.
Antarctica's exhaustion mounted up.
Tears froze when tea iced over in the cup.
Men watched their spangled, shivering souls depart.

Scott's duty drove them through his diary's ice.
Imperishable footprints! – Stone boots plod
On endless journeys to a brutish God
In expeditionary paradise

Where *Terra Nova*, in auroral light,
Waits like warm heaven on a packed ice-field.
'*To strive, to seek, to find, and not to yield*' –
Men vanished in the blizzards of goodnight.

Self-sacrificial 'Soldier' Oates lies there
Still sinking down the ice-cap draped in breath
That turned to crystals when he welcomed death.
He's shrouded in refrigerated prayer.

Tay-craftsmen built their ships. One ship survives
Whale-days of carpentry and masted glades,

Forgotten tradesmen, half-remembered trades
Echoing down a century of lives.

A girl in service wiped her steamed-up glass
In Broughty Ferry as a ship sailed by
Equipped to seek, and then solemnify
Adventure's flag on a white landmass

Where elbows, memories and fingers froze,
Stopped in the simple act of picking up
Gratitude's tea in its Edwardian cup
When life solidified in mouth and nose.

Vainglorious Scott's no image for our science
And arts; but think about devotion, or
How Captain Oates in human metaphor
Describes selflessness, and defiance.

What did *she* feel watching *Discovery*'s
Departure? Probably nothing, as steam
Re-clouded the window – she, too, a dream,
Or less than that, in the world's stories.

Parrot Islands

Let there be room still for utmost Utopias,
For the back of beyond and the cobbled quays,
The boy and the one-legged pirate, wind-stoked canvas,
Adventure, delight, and doing whatever you please.
In a world of endpaper maps and clear-cut surprise,
There should be such chances, in a world without lies.

Room, too, for maritime visions, the Seven Seas'
Pollutionless stretches that wander for miles and miles
Over unsignposted distance, the primitive breeze
Driving the schooner to the Kingdom of Smiles;
And space for the legend of the journey and quest
Then straight home to bed and the one you love best.

Pink above turquoise, and purple clouds darkening,
Here is 'another sky', beautiful, local, and true.
Someone is dreaming it, a mind on its wing
In search of the life that comes out of the blue.
Ah, Stevenson, your pages pleased me as a boy.
Now that I'm not, I weep over them, and with joy.

'Contemporary Scottish Writing'

'Wahnt ony bizniz?' shouts a whore
Fun-furred among her pack of whüres,
One leaning on a puke-stained door –
A far cry from the Lammermuirs.

Agates

Chateau d'Yquem-coloured, Arran-shaped, terraced
For viniculture, its semi-precious bays
Wait for the never-arriving ornamented boat.
Others are silver, turquoise, red, blue,
Eyes, circles, locked, lapidary vistas
Invented by volcanic accidents.

What draws me to them? Is it words like agate,
Jasp, chalcedony, carnelian, onyx,
Or names of where they came from and can be found? –
Balmerino, Glen Farg, and Scurdie Ness,
Balmeadowside, Iona, and St Cyrus ...
Whatever – they are all pieces of universe.

1996

The Expelair in the lavatory –
Relentless thing – is a better orator
Than I would want to be. A piece of grit
Adds whingeing to its sucked-out smell of shit.
The same old switched-on stinking story –
Rhetoric, excrement. Better by far
A peach tree's blossom in its world of window
Which asks no questions as to why or how
Silence suffers in its empty city where
Stenches of grief defeat its Expelair.

Sunrise

Evanishments are everywhere and not,
Not here, not now, when smoked red steps
Out of the sea into
Split-second visible thunder.

First light. The moment of day.
Childhood of light and geography.
Last legs of moonlight dangle from a roof.
Near shapes totter into their names.

They shift from strangeness into domesticity.
Night shrinks into corners under trees.
It will crawl like fugitives all day
Through conifers, wounded by birdsong and breezes.

A solitary star is *Good-morning, Good-morning,*
Good-morning in fictitious light.
Its displaced radiance is caught by a daisy.
It is a tear of drinkable dew.

Incalculable fire slides from the sea
And a universe invades my privacy.
It belittles me.
The first swallows are up and flying.

The world is a clear coastline.
There are no departures or goodbyes.
Place and the big river are sleepless,
A borderland where sight gives up its ghosts.

Art is Wonderful

Now that you've found us, strip. Yes, naked. Please.
No one can see you. No, you aren't 'safe'.
Yes, everything, including socks and shoes.

You're feeling humble? Walk into Room One.
Before you ask, the man you see there is
Well and truly stuffed, and no effigy.

He's an oboeist-ideologue of 1937.
Beside him in the glass case you can see
Corrected flutes and censored violins,

A Red tuba and an Aryan clarinet.
That pickled larynx in the little jar
Belonged to a dictator's diva.

The room itself 's conflated from thirteen
Bunkered boudoirs, while that gramophone
Raved with sophisticated folklore as

Its owner plotted on strategic maps
And inspiration dug millions of graves.
That, as you know, is what you're listening to –

Countless busy amateur undertakers.
National epics are death certificates.
It's a lucky country that doesn't have them.

Room Two contains unpublished libraries,
Secret editions, and artists' farewell notes
Spotted with tears. Hence the noiseless fountain.

In spaces between silent anthems, you'll hear
Solitary shots in the back of the neck
And the consciences of conscripts in firing squads.

No, nothing in Room Three. Nothing. Except
An exile's sigh. Nothing at all. Nothing
Other than nocturnal human noise, farts,

Feet shuffling in dust, a child's cry,
A scream out of an unforgotten rape
Trying to find its home in a footnote.

In Four, however, study the withered bouquets
On the wall hung also with ballet shoes.
Listen to all those recorded bravos.

In Five, observe demented gargoyles
Dismantled from Party architecture.
Now you can understand why nakedness

Means something as you stand before
Mass-murderers portrayed in lousy oils
Or the once ubiquitous office photographs.

Backbiting poets turned each other in
To cultural police, and here you have them
Preserved in Six. Yes, more than you thought.

Those were the days of the Denounced Concerto
And states of mind that led directly to
Drudgery, death, and through the guarded gates.

Room Seven, therefore, is dedicated to
Honesty, fidelity, and humiliation.
We convey this through sub-zero temperatures,

The smell of sweat, ordure, and decomposition.
It is all written down. Nothing is lost.
Be warned by this. Your microphoned ambition

Gives off much the same aroma, and so, too, does
Detestable fame-footwork smack of the same
Dishonest, selfish choreography.

And now, enjoy the spectacle of The Arts
In their moods of 'Health Through Strength',
'A Day Down on the Collective Farm',

'With the Heroic Construction Crews at X',
'I Painted This to Make Lots of Money'.
Room Eight is complicated but depressing.

Room Nine is just meant to remind you.
Hence the exhibits of unsculpted stone,
Colours, pencils, paper, and instruments,

Alphabets, tools, wood, the notes of the scales,
An empty stage, Comedy, and Tragedy.
Room Nine is the Unvarnished Truth. Love it.

Room Ten is your room. Do not leave the room
As you find it. Make your mark on its walls.
It is not defacement to write on them.

It is up to you what you choose.
Why do you need to ask? LIBERTY. ART.
BEAUTY. TRUTH. They're all lying to hand.

They're charms against terror's arithmetic.
They'll preserve you from stupidity.
They'll make your life difficult, your work true.

Leave by the door ahead of you. Your clothes
Will be found where you left them. Hurry.
No. You can't come back. Don't attempt it.

Be quick. Another is waiting.
No, as I said, you can't return here.
Do I need to say everything twice?

Another is waiting. Another is always waiting.
You chose. Don't complain of your life.
There are no second chances. That is the point.

Teachers

*Mrs Margaret Espinasse, the staff of the English Department,
University of Hull, 1966–1969, and Philip Larkin, University
Librarian*

A Jacobite in a Franconian *schloss*;
White Russian countess sponging in Shanghai
While editing the S.T.S.'s *Ross* . . .
Beowulf's auntie, Viking samurai! . . .
Now that you're fiction, lady, I don't want
Inaccuracies creeping in, by front,
Back, or side doors. I want your scholarship,
Philology, your charm, here in my lines,
Your politics, helping me give the slip
To what oppress me, to my depressions.

The Anglo-Saxon poetry abattoir –
Cross-gartered louts whose metrical panache
Struck me at first as dire, the verse of scar,
Heroic, armoured, but mere cut and slash,
You taught me how to like, and then to love
Its helmeted alliterative shove.
You taught me, too, how to enjoy digression.
'To Hull's and Scotland's weather, you should say
– And this, believe me, 's an important lesson –
"Do what you like, because I live today".'

'Read Chaucer to the full, but know our own.
Henryson, Douglas and Dunbar – for us,
Indigenous poetry needn't be homespun.
They'll form our confidential syllabus.'
I used to write at night. My tiny desk
Felt crowded if I dropped an asterisk.

Venus was thair present ... O cruell Saturne ...
O dulfull harp! ... Mine hert was not in pes.
The room was cold and dark; I felt it burn.
I wepit for myne wife Erudices.

Night after night, trying each umpteenth Muse
For suitability, a Scots accord
Between my accent and a verbal bruise
Inflicted on each cadenced English word
In an attempt to write the way I spoke
Reduced your protégé to an *Inglis* joke.
'Put your pen where your mouth is. Feel your mouth
Speak through your nib ...' Good, dangerous advice ...
Study, study, burning the last of youth.
Who'd guess its cost in studious sacrifice!

Postscripted, synthesized, yesterday's lyric
Was sonic archaeology, Scots voice
From way-back-when whose victory is pyrrhic
Now, closed to openness, chance, change and choice.
My mouth felt numb. Words, words! My mouth and nib
Mumbled and scratched within a *Scottis* fib.
'*Thaes ofereode, thisses swa maege,*' you said.
'Scotland's not over, but its tongue's been lost.'
I felt ashamed. I wanted to be dead.
'We speak our *Inglis* through a *Scottis* ghost.'

You taught me how to speak and be at ease
With accent, self, and love of literature.
Now I can do whatever I damn well please
With my rolled *r*, hard *l*, and hurried slur
In my parish phonology, my own lilt,
My father's voice, but not ancestral guilt,
Nor blotted mouth, nor metaphrastic pen

Translating how I speak to how I don't,
Into one tongue and then back out again.
'Good, then, to learn to don't do what you won't!'

Love above all, its who, its when and where
Melting in local light and circumstance,
Can find their meaning in *my* lyric care –
Not politics only, but time and chance,
Reality's garden, no scunner in it,
The indefinite and the infinite
In a large phrase. And all that's what I want,
Beginning in a language I can trust
As mine, live in it, hide there, sing, or flaunt,
Not what I'm told to say, but what I must.

Pleasure intrigues me, and a memory is
Part of my hedonism's source, reaching back
To hear and see a lovely helpfulness
Which tries to cure a pain in present lack,
My dear, dead Mrs Espinasse, whose time
Spent with me helped me with my crippled rhyme.
'It's a vocation. I don't have it, though
They tell me Mr Larkin has. *His* Muse,
Now ... *There's* an oddity! A very low
Unbardic poet. A talent to bemuse.

'A poet who *administers*, who sits on
Committees! ... Colloquial, but mark
Some of the stranger passages he hits on
Sound and sing beyond the scribbles of a clerk
Between meetings.' *If you could see me now!*
Better behind an eighteenth-century plough
Than what I do, inheriting the Toad,
The thirst, but not the gift. Rather 'toad *work*'

[28]

Than 'toad *poetry*', or that the unhallowed
Oppress me. Who'd be a sixty-year-old jerk

In jeans and leather going from hall to hall
With book in hand, and upping up the fee,
Reciting yourself, from Falkirk to Walsall?
Far too demanding. Too much like work for me.
I did it, and admit – Larkin was right!
You lose more than you gain when you recite.
One way or another, you dig your grave.
You choose, and do, and that's your epitaph.
Lucky for you, if you don't misbehave
And leave behind the present of a laugh.

A Complete Stranger

Whatever's said about the cause of it,
I'm left with a train's cry and puzzled sorrow.
Mechanical emergency's blare
Sang with the horror that the driver saw.
Another is a woman's soft, faint thud
On the run out of Stroud in October –
Trim houses, leafy gardens, laden pear trees,
Purple multitudes of unpicked damsons.
I was thinking of fruit when it happened.
'A well-known suicide spot,' someone said,
And the remark was taken up by young women
Complaining of the selfishness of suicides.
Whatever's said, whatever, by police,
Coroners, or those in grievous surprise,
Two sensations are filed in me.
One is a train's klaxon crying.
One is a minor shock in my arthritic knee.
'Why so long?' 'Why can't we go?'
Policemen walked up and down the train.
Their radios were a source of other voices.
A man with a portable radio telephone
Rearranged his self-important day.
People craned to see the dead woman.
There was nothing to see. She was being protected.
So, there was an end to someone's story.
Her face is written on the driver's eyes.
('They'll have to replace him. We'll need another.')
Her last breath is in my sensitive knee.
I shall have to apologize for lateness.
I must resist saying why. I am sorry.

I knew her only as an anonymous thud –
And as pears, damsons, and speculations –
As a complete stranger, and as this.

Three Poets

I

It was a very bad year for the deaths of poets –
*Norman MacCaig, Sorley MacLean, and George Mackay
Brown.*
Then everybody move up one? No, it's
All drop down and kiss the ground
For the lyric scourge of hypocrites,
The bardic master, the voice of an Orcadian town.

Disturbed anthologies! *Momento mori* –
*George Mackay Brown, Norman MacCaig, and Sorley
MacLean.*
They died in the same year! A tripled cry
In metrical, thrice-measured sound
Praises the biggest man of Skye,
The earl of Hamnavoe, and the prince of the humane.

Three great men lost within one lousy year! –
*Sorley MacLean, George Mackay Brown, Norman
MacCaig.*
Words feel disordered and they can't cohere
Unless to toast truly crowned
Dead verse-heroes, but not in beer –
No, by *George, Norman, and Sorley*, we won't be vague!

II

Norman, when asked, 'Norman, do you smoke?'
Answered politely with his polished joke –
'Almost professionally.' Norman, I do, too,
As you knew, and as you said was 'good for me'

Although I'm not so sure. I'm not like you.
A lung of mine *barks*, and it scans *spondee*.

Norman, when asked, 'Norman, do you drink?'
Thought for a second, and said, 'Do I *think*?'
Then when the malt was poured, the hostess said,
'Would you like something in it?' Norman stared.
'Another tilt of *that* pure thoroughbred
Glen Grant, and water, please, and then I'm watered.'

Norman, a handsome man, adored ladies,
Who adored him. He loved the Hebrides.
He loved Assynt, warblers, stonechats, dry-stane dykes,
Small lochs with herons – so, put it about,
He was a man of more likes than dislikes –
Friends, ladies, swans, toads, cormorants, and trout.

What Norman *didn't* like, Norman *detested*
With wit such as could get a man arrested –
For cut-price academics, pedants, bores,
Or sanctimonious swine – his lethal ire! –
Or frauds, or politicians who cause wars.
Lyric intelligence, but ringed with fire!

III

'Keep left', he used to say, 'Keep left', meaning
'Get off my right-hand side, it's deaf',
As well as something political, as if
I might have faltered in my own leaning
To the left side of intellect, the left
Frontier and margin of mind's craft and drift.

In Austria – Sorley, Eddie, Liz, and me,
British Council-ing – three poets trembled for

[33]

Sorley, that old 'don't talk about the war'
Punctilio, knowing what will be will be,
And, knowing Sorley, what you could predict –
Six feet and eighty years of self-respect,

His warrior Gaelic verse, its ancestry
In a thousand stories, valorous big blades
Swinging through battles, feuds and cattle raids,
And no hint of remorse or sophistry.
Pre-supermarket, Sorley, you'd no choice
Other than Gaelic's unsurrendered voice.

Like Lovat's soldiers speaking Gaelic over
Open radio, your language fell on ears
Still puzzled after forty-something years
By melodies that sounded like an undercover
Elusive code, a tongue no German knew,
And music, not the meaning, getting through.

I like to think of one of Rommel's men
Listening in to Gaelic conversation
Through earphones in the desert, listening in,
A wondering philologist, his pen
Jotting phonetics, then, closing his eyes,
Hears sea and islands and Atlantic skies.

IV

Your fragrance finished, but your love and lore
Survive in your inscribed and lovely verse.
I never met a man, George, who knew more
Truth than you did, or felt less for commerce.

Iconic, weathered, Nordic, proud, and calm ...
You were your own epoch. You were your own.
Your sculpted lyric and your runic psalm
Came from a world before the telephone,

Modernity, TV, and apparatus –
From your domain of faith's handwritten craft,
Orcadian sky, Orcadian afflatus,
The truths and histories you epitaphed.

V

Depleted poetry! The tides still ebb and flow,
Rose-clouds pinken, hills are white with year-end snow.
But ah! the naked birch trees and the frosted grass,
The weather-sorrow measured on the weatherglass,
The winking lights, diminished day, the river flowing,
A robin on the climbing-frame, the darkness growing
As nineteen ninety-six gets put away and time
Aches to the measures of posterity and rhyme.

A large subtraction from our triple-tongued sublime!
Come, we should listen to the shadows, to the light,
To peat becoming ash in the lyrical night
As it darkens to deepest splendour, as flames climb
In the lum and the indoor pine's baubles swing and chink
In a strange draught. Come, friends, it is time now to drink
To three poets. It is time to sit quietly and read,
Hearing them speak their lines, those whom we succeed,

Our chiefs of men, our leaders in the spirit of us,
Those whom we loved for showing us the wit of us.
Drink, then, with a full heart, with gratitude, saying
Their poetry aloud as if we are praying
To the Muse of our country, asking her to guide us,
To keep us true and triple, not to divide us
Into pathetic factions set on matricide.
Lady, guide us. Re-teach us dignity and pride.

Come, friends, it is time now to drink to three poets.
Let us raise our glasses to those who strengthened our wits.
Come, friends, let us drink to our nation's finest men.
Let us drink to them. Then let us drink to them again.

The Black Douglas

Time, now, for a sojourn in a big cave
On any Celtic island – Jura, Rathlin –
Watching a spider swing on its gut-woven
Life-support system until it gets there.
Or to linger over cups in Luvian's,
The Aero Café, Ma Brown's, or The Tav,
Looking for the same moment of decision
Which is whatever it is I have to decide.
Doubtless, I'll think of something in due course.
Then I'll go back to work. Always, it involves
Riding against the enemy. This time
I'll throw the casketed hearts of my dead friends
And then I'll throw my own, shouting 'Hurrah!
This is my choice taken by pure decision!
This is my gesture discussed with myself
Watching a spider or over cups of coffee.'
They won't be impressed. Therefore, I'll ride on
Into the glade of swords, yelling 'Scotland!
I'm doing my best and my worst! Hallelujah!'

Woodnotes

Looking into a wood, the mind gets lost
In complicated sameness, on and on.
Senses grow green and wooden. My own ghost
Waves from ground-misted ferns, and then it's gone
In half the time it takes to blink. Mind, leaf,
Life, mist, stop together in the soft clock
Within me, caught on thorns of disbelief
And welcome, as a life's *tick-tock, tick-tock*
Delivers its involuntary beats
Into an unthinned forest's olive light
Clammy with earth-locked rain, high summer heat's
Low airlessness, dusk dwindling into night.

A selfish, inner, pleasurable fright
Lasting no time at all, or man-shaped mist,
Botanic fog, a kind of second-sight,
A trick of light that says I, too, exist –
Whatever incommunicable threat
Stood in the ferns and waved – knowable fate,
Momento mori or my spirit's sweat
Evaporating – I saw my duplicate.
Abject but happy with the sight I saw
I stood and sniffed the stink of my remorse
Flow from my years and deeds, fault laced with flaw,
A silent, sniffing, waving, grinning discourse.

Silence like music that must not be played,
A score that must be read with the body posed
At a forbidden instrument, dismayed
Hands locked above potential music closed
To its performance – play it in the mind,

An abstract symphony releasing real
Ethical harmonies until they're signed
As what you cannot say but what you feel.
In a birdless forest where no fresh winds blow
I saw my other stand among the ferns
And what I didn't know I got to know
And what I learned is what a dead man learns.

Oblivion at an instant's open door –
The green of it, my whole life running past –
And then I was back again, the forest's floor
Greener than ever in the hemmed-in vast
Confinedness of the wood. I waved back
At where I'd been while being where
I'd seen him/me. A leaf dripped and a black
Defoliated tree creaked like my chair
But quietly so that only I could hear
(Or so I thought) its phrases of dead wood
Dismiss themselves; but what they meant was clear –
Revise your life, and use your solitude.

Exilic, but the root still strong and deep,
The feeling hurt me but a gratitude
Rose up within me and a big upsweep
Of thoughts I can't describe but wish I could.
I felt fictitious, shoved into a realm
Outside quotidian experience
For grey-green light and mist to overwhelm
In a self-haunted, near-nocturnal rinse,
As of the end of something, or of me
And what I've done, and what I do, a stop.
Cool darkness shivered in that leafless tree.
A drip formed on a fern. I watched it drop.

A tiny noise. Water descending from
One leaf to another in the laddered air
And if you listen hard there is rhythm
To this belated rain on the green stair
Down to the damp ground, and it is as if
Water is careful, and leaves are careful too,
Helping each other on the leaf-cupped cliff
That is existence, down from the high blue
Through the green, and into the supporting earth.
To work this out would show me as a fraud –
All life's design as birth, and then rebirth.
It takes more than religion to make God.

Leopardi

Natura con un pugno lo sgobbò:
'Canta', gli disse irata; ed ei cantò.

Niccolò Tommaseo

What makes us say a thing is beautiful
Or some one, too, is lovely, such as you?
Devotion that's beyond the dutiful
Or truth superior to the merely true –
These, too, excite us. No one can explain
Melodic mysteries written down but wrung
First from the dishrag of a poet's pain
Before a word of it gets thought and sung.

Poets are lucky whose deformities
Are visible as humps upon their backs,
Byronic clubfoot or Miltonic blindness,
Clinical mania, dipsomaniac
Rage and staggers. Others make do with this
Inward sensation of hurt, a disfigured
Moment no longer knowable, noesis
Through imagination. But Tommaseo sniggered.

And that was *his* deformity. Who reads
Niccolò Tommaseo? When satire's thorns
Crown virtue it's the satirist who bleeds
In footnote after footnote. No one mourns
Wrong critics or those poets who sought fame
Through disregard of sorrow, high regard
For 'confidence', 'performance', the acclaim
Enshrined in dire normality's blowhard

Perfections, the 'politically correct'
Anticipation of the well anticipated.
Leopardi, a well and truly wrecked
Poet from birth, unhappy, and unmated,
Library child, aristocrat, you dug deep
Into deformity, as I dig deep
In mine, so as to write to you, and keep
Faith with your sorrows, ugliness, pain, keep

Faith with the art of poetry submerged
In its reviled soil of self and famished
Desires, its rankness, horrors and its dirged
Humanity, its status of the banished.
My soul is very dirty. Yours was, too.
So, too, is everyone's, especially those
Who claim theirs aren't. Leopardi, you,
A semi-crippled student of the rose,

Fireflies, and your own spine, dear dust, I call
To you across the years from my own sickness
With the *buon giorno* of my kind and all
Best wishes from your over-aged apprentice.
Big spirit, little man – your voice sings on
In its encyclopaedic solitude,
Lyrical intellect, best read when dawn
Floods on the curtains with its fortitude.

To 'purify the soul' ... Sooner attempt
To make the world kind as purify
Whatever soul means. Poetry's exempt
From such theology. Its lyric cry
Cries that self is sagacious, worldly, sore,
Particular, and selfish, but benign.

Not much is new in it. All's as before –
Sung intellect and feeling, line by line

In tune with life, life-love and temperament,
Truth and its poetry in the accord
Life strikes with tuneful saying, like a scent
Arising from the sound of each clear word
In an eccentric harmony, a true
Sound-of-who, bias-of-self, nitty-gritty
Gist-of-poet, smell-of-who, the 'I', the 'you',
Submergence of them in the sense and pity

A poem makes for the world in which we live.
When a full moon drives highways of light over
Broad, potent Tay, my poets are talkative.
Archival spirits, lunar, undercover,
'God's spies', indeed, I listen to the night's
Fogged, morbid estuarial blue, and hear
Best poetry's etceteras, birthright's
Language – Rilke, you, Milton, and Shakespeare,

Keats, Byron, Browning, Auden, Burns, and so
I am kept sane by dreaming voices, moons,
And the stars' echoes, and the sleeping sparrow,
Buzzless hive-hidden bees, a lonely spoon's
Reflection of a star cupped in its cup
Like curative liquid, and a sense of art
Which says its purpose is to raise soul up
While also pleasing us, and breaking the heart.

Pushkin's Ring

*He took with him a gold talisman-ring with a cabbalistic Hebrew
inscription, which Countess Verontsova had slipped onto his
finger one day after they had made love on a Black Sea beach.
Pushkin wore the ring for the rest of his life. It was removed by
friends after his death thirteen years later in a duel, and survived
until 1917 when an unknown looter took it from the Pushkin
Museum in Moscow in the early months of the Revolution.*

Neal Ascherson, *Black Sea*

Such is the history of gold, one ring
Appears a trifle in the greedy archive.
Imagine his friends' sorrowful smiles
When they tugged it over the knuckle
Or held it to a lamp or window, squinting
To read the lucky and protective marks
Which didn't save him from the pistol shot
Aimed by the foppish Baron. Lodged in
Pushkin's belly, the bullet left him time
To think and die, remembering Onegin
And Lensky in the snow, how poetry
Foretells and feeds on future sorrow.
But it's a splendid story, is it not? –
The real and the fictitious poet shot
By a literary, echoic bullet;
The glass-cased ring, which lovers, scholars,
Readers, peered at, curators' anecdotes;
A travelling poet staring hard at what
Commemorated Pushkin's seaside love
And lived against his skin like a woman.
Odd, then, that one loved by the people should

Find his ghost looted, but the desecration
Means little in eternity, although
I can't help thinking of its movement through
History, like those primary school essays –
'Adventures of a Penny', 'The Lost Thimble'.
In mine the penny went from purse to pocket,
Pocket to purse, from Duke to roadsweeper
And all round everywhere until it found
A beggar on Jamaica Bridge, whose life
It saved by buying him a piece of bread.
Pushkin's ring, too, could have been a godsend
To someone with a starving family
Or its theft commissioned by a connoisseur
Who craved to wear the ring the poet wore.
Pawned, hawked, or touted, it could have moved through
Revolutionary commerce, finding its home
On a tasteful Jewish man's finger, who liked
Its Hebrew inscription, perhaps, by now,
In Łodz, or Riga, or Kiev, removed
When lining up with others in a camp
Or at a ditch-side in a forest clearing,
Thieved, or threaded on a long string with others,
Smelted, made into bullion, gold death-bricks
Lodged in the secret vaults of Switzerland
Or transacted between God-knows-who
Among parked cars on a dark Alpine road,
A grimly European rendezvous
Where wicked history converts to cash.
There could be many other fantasies
Invented to describe what happened to
Pushkin's ring – for these things happen, not often,
As Gogol said, but it's a fact, they do.
From time to time, the answers are outrageous.

What you imagine could be true! Suppose
It found its way to Boris Pasternak,
Or Anna Ahkmatova, Marina Tsvetaeva,
Or Osip Mandel'shtam. Suppose it was
On Mandel'shtam's finger when *he* died,
And no one noticed, no one took it off.
Suppose it's somewhere near Vladivostok
In the ground, around a poet's bone digit.
Suppose Joseph Brodsky found it in New York.
Suppose *I* have it. Suppose I'm wearing it
Right now. For that would be appropriate,
Having lost another ring, having lost it
Because of poetry, being married to it.
Pushkin would understand. He was a good bloke.
He would have understood the pain, hunger,
Passion, cruelty, anguish, in all of it.
As long as he's remembered, he'd forgive
Posterity's Judas. He'd see the joke.

If Only

It was at a moment of Lambrettas
On Eastwoodmains Road, where I stood
Under a laburnum, waiting for her.

Rich kids revved on their machines
And I'd just finished work in the library.
It was 8 p.m. and the suburb glowed with prosperity.

I'd my raincoat over my arm and felt stupid
Not to be motorized or in tennis whites,
Earning £5 a week and working the late shift.

Dust on the pavement mixed with
Dropped petals and litter. A bee buzzed
In my ear, a yellow interlude.

It was a moment of swallows and evening sunlight
On the Tennis Club roof, a moment
Populated by sports cars and resentment.

My mind was far gone in lyrical grudges
Drowning in leaf-music and panic –
'What shall I do? What's my future?'

And she ran towards me, hot from tennis.
I couldn't believe it. I was so happy.
I'd expected to wait for ever

Or until a policeman ordered me away.
I think I'm still there, haunting a gutter.
If only I knew then what I still don't know.

On Whether Loneliness Ever Has a Beginning

I

'For all my errors,
I've been always
In love, always,
With someone or other.'

And I remember Gaye,
Elspeth, Jean, and Mhairi,
Diane and Lorna, Myra,
The girls of my boyhood.

Wireless songs come back
From the 40s and 50s,
From etherized bakelite –
'Blue Moon', 'It's Too Soon to Know'.

I see a girl by the palings
Pretending to smoke
Confectionary cigarettes,
Wearing her mother's shoes.

'Red Sails in the Sunset'
'Sunny Side of the Street'
'I Hadn't Anyone Till You'
'Into Each Life Some Rain Must Fall'

II

I walked a girl from school
Carrying her briefcase,
Talking of books and teachers
On Paisley's pavements.

'I could walk you home.'
'It's impossible,' she said.
'I live in Kilmacolm.'
She left me at the station.

Out on my bicycle
I saw her with her parents
Picknicking near Formakin.
Their car was black and Bentley.

I slowed and waved.
Her mother looked angry.
The girl waved slowly to me.
It was the wave of one meaning goodbye.

III

At school, a girl who liked me
Was tall and religious.
The lamp on her green badge
Proclaimed 'Scripture Union'.

'Well, no, I don't attend
Bible Class. I went twice.
I fell out with it.
I have very serious doubts.'

Or so I said, after
Reading Shelley for a month
And still at Lirici
Stirring poetic embers.

Hot spirit was my fad then,
Atheistical glory
And soaring grievance,
Pyre of a rasping soul.

A teacher told us we looked well together –
Girls' Captain of Sanda House,
Boys' Captain of Sanda House,
Fit as athletic fiddles.

I ran the last lap
In the relay, and didn't win it.
She jumped up and down in her white shorts.
She ran, and did the same.

God got in the way
And I can't remember her name,
Not even with my mnemonic
Sixth Year class photograph

Or her voice saying,
'I *can't* go out with a heathen.
So why won't you come to church with me?
Why are you so obstinate?'

IV

At Norma's house
On the first patio
In Paisley, bottles –
Sauternes – bobbed in a pail,

White enamel,
And like a little sea,
Bobbing, bobbing,
One, two, three.

'Peggy Sue', 'Rock Around the Clock'
'Long Tall Sally'
'Hail, Hail Rock 'n' Roll' –
Sweet wine was the taste of those days.

[50]

There was a smell –
New cement, chrysanthemums,
Perfume and strawberries –
And the sound of twaddle

As someone talked about
Existentialism and Sartre.
Goodbye, my generation!
I seem to have walked out on you

A long time ago
And into my own life.
Is that what it took
To have to write a book or two

Where we come from?
Or you walked out on me.
I haven't heard from you.
You haven't heard from me.

I do this for us,
For Juliette Greco,
Simone de Beauvoir,
Jean-Paul Sartre, Albert Camus,

And for you, too,
Whose names have gone
From me, into a cloud
Hanging over me.

v

I met her in the library
At Giffnock, where I worked.
She wanted Leonard Feather's
Encyclopedia of Jazz.

She wanted to look up
Victor Feldman.
It was a Friday in September
Forty years ago.

Time passes, or doesn't,
On the wristwatch she gave me
Four years later.
The life it's measured!

I still wear it.
It keeps *excellent* time.
It will be by my bedside
On the day I die.

Older, and no wiser,
I sit in the sun
With understanding
That's always on the edge

Nearing its conclusions,
Always getting closer
But never reaching
What I want to know.

All I can think of
Are the ties I've owned,
Shoes, jackets, pens –
But somehow, especially, ties –

As if this means something
And I've lost myself
On a coathanger
Or mislaid my address.

VI

Many years go by,
Marriages, children,
Holidays, couplings,
Laughter, tears.

One died. Another
Employs her lawyer,
And here I am
Talking to myself

But not listening –
The lonely breakfast,
Small supper,
Acrid cigarette.

Annotating shadows,
Textures, chair squeaks,
Small domestic hums,
I am getting to know

Solitude inside out,
From all angles.
I compose still lifes –
Oranges, bananas,

Apples, grapes, pears,
Books, pens, more books,
Paper, a bottle,
And then I eat them.

VII

I eat responsibility.
I eat work and budgets.

I toil in my garden,
Sometimes even at night.

After my daughter visits
There is colossal silence.
It is my silence.
It comes from within me.

Do you remember
Castelvecchio Pascoli
And silence on the bridge,
A stream running through it,

And glowworms lit
On the path ahead of us?
It is that silence.
There is a noise in it.

And the graveyard
With the lit candles
And gladioli?
Why did we die?

Love doesn't die.
It's like a country.
I pray to a star —
Sharp, cold, and clear.

VIII

Another silence haunts me
From La Peyrière, Tursac,
Among fragrances of limes.
The noise is of trees rustling.

Neither silence is better.
They are the same, and mine.
They are in my memory.
I know them to the letter.

Except that there is no 'letter'
For these silences live
Only in mind and memory's
Cerebral, wordless hive.

How does love begin? –
Because it does.
Why does love end? –
It doesn't end.

Without moving my lips,
Without moving my tongue,
In my mouthless silence
I listen to my own cry.

IX

Now, though, I possess
Particular silence.
I look out on
Nocturnal hillsides

From where my garden ends
And solitude blows back
In my face like something
Sensed but unseen.

A fox stops and looks at me,
Pityingly, then goes off
On its reddish trot,
Bushy-tailed, real, not thought,

In the half-frosted moonlight,
Very clear, the pale blue wash
Of starlight, woods clearing
To my adjusted eyes

And one star dancing on
A sumach's antlers,
Another in my eye,
And still the world stays sacred

In its local reach,
A place's temperament,
Its magic stretching back
Into the dim and distant

Realities beyond
What happens to us –
All these surprise me
As I stand and smoke

In the cold dark
At 2 a.m. in January
Still keeping true
To some belief or other

I don't know much about
And have no name for.
I'll go in soon
And try to sleep.

March 13, 1994

Having heard nothing from you for some time
Makes all the difference. Things look worse today
And if doves call in their contented tunefulness
A guttered apple-core looked very ugly
On the sunless side of North Street, teeth-marks
Edged with bacterial rust, road-grit sticking
To its dried juice and bitten fruit flavours.
What's on at the Picture House? I looked and saw.
That, too, was unappetizing. Later on,
My black coffee was an odious darkness,
A liquid without light, a sour drink.
I thought of the apple-core, then you, remote,
Wordless, beyond alphabets and telephones.
You don't even remember me. How can you?
There are distances farther than miles and silence.
I'll go there. Each day I'm inching closer.
What's on the menu? Is it too expensive?

You

You won't believe it. Perhaps you're too prosaic
    To fall for a poetic ache,
But your smile (when you smile), your eyes, your nose,
    Are far too beautiful for prose.

Don't credit this, my dear, if you don't want to.
    A poem, too, can be a pack of lies.
But if you don't, then I'll come back and haunt you.
    You'll find me hard to exorcise.

Native Meditation

At midnight in the sitting-room, lights off,
TV off, in the aroma of log-light
With a large dram crystalled, and more than enough
To last the darkness of a philosophic night,
I contemplate how timber turns to ash
In a wintry fire. An energetic flame,
Rising and dying, rising, domestic dash
Uttered in hearth-light, speaks of love and shame,
A lonely, lyric husbandry of thought
And poetry, the curse of scholarship,
Work's albatross, this bitter, native sip
That is a liquid and ancestral cry
From thermal waters made in the year dot –
This hearth-flame rises and it will not die.

Night Watch

Parsing this silence is listening to wood.
Sky and the moon's off-yellow golden highway
Sprinkle across sleepless, nocturnal Tay –
Firth, stars, accessories of solitude.
Familiar rooftops, treetops, closing in
On the window, no longer protect me.
Birch, box, wall, and the skyline reject me,
And the parish breaks as sweat on my skin
As I watch the pulsing of my Gatsby-light
On the Angus shore. How many tons of Tay
Pass silently as I say this, careless,
Waiting? Any minute now, and the night
Will start to lighten as ounces of day
Seep from the sea's exhausted genesis.

Dinner

Hungry for too long, the first hot spoonful
Juddered me with its sudden soothe and taste.
I huddled over the aroma of minestrone
As if in a soup kitchen in a charity coat,
Thankful and blessed by circumstance while also
Alert to my companion's dainty attack,
He being well fed, quicker, his expectations
Satisfied to the minute in his happier routines.
Slowly, with gratitude, I emptied the plate,
Wiped it with bread, drank down my wine and water.
I could eat no more, nor ordered it.
My companion did, he with the appetite,
Security and confident conversation.
He was too hungry, or not hungry enough,
Ignorant of the gluttonies of aloneness
Which are frugal fare, the small meal prepared,
Half-eaten, cleared away, the empty table,
Four hopeful chairs, and life without kiss.

Out of Breath

Of the Cardiff Empire Games of '58
My memory's a black-and-white ten-inch screen
On a succession of Inchinnan afternoons –
Joe Connolly's six miles, Harry Fenion's marathon,
Two Bellahouston Harriers running for Scotland.
Our club's vest with the blue saltire said I, too,
Might take their place and be breathless for a flag.
And Herb Elliot, whose skull-close haircut I copied,
'Playing the sedulous ape' to an improbable talent
And wearing it again like a demented toupée ...
I'm returning in the way of a man who's been ill
In search of an inexpressibly wise sentence
Lost among the spoken paragraphs of a lifetime.
Milka Singh, the running Indian, whose tilt,
Fast lope and long hair in a knot tied to a flower,
Remain fixed as aromatic memories –
Cardamom, coriander, and rain at dusk,
Colours of saffron, small peppers, turmeric –
Revisits four hundred and forty yards of fortitude;
Or Brian Hewson, 'the head waiter', ruined
By Elliot's second lap in forty-nine seconds.
Ambition's puff, the sheer try of it, comes down,
In the end, to self-defeat – so much shed sweat,
Sore muscles, but still, 'internal exile', frontiers
Within the body that can't be crossed, even with
Effort's mania driving on into the opposite
Exertion to the one rehearsed with physical
Dedication on vanished lanes and meadows,
In chainsawed woodlands and on old cinder tracks.
I feel short of breath, as if I've measured it.

Sedentary, aware of vanquishment and reverse,
Whelmed by whisky, tobacco, by choice of work,
On a hiding to nothing, I choose to continue with
Pathetic and pious poetry in which victory
Can only ever be a passage of words. An art
In which adversity is a matter of fact and form,
Valour a way of saying, triumph but small bucks
And laurels less exposed than an Olympian's,
Verse is my adult, short-legged, long-winded game
In which shame fights it out with posterity.
At least I can remember breasting the tape (twice)
Which is what I do now as I take from a box
My old Bellahouston blue vest, its blue saltire,
My white 'County' vest with its Renfrewshire badge,
My red Adidas track shoes with the white stripes.
In touching them I touch a lost identity
In order to meditate on incomplete
Accomplishment, on mind and body, endeavour,
Fatigue, and desolation. It sounds too extreme,
On the verge of morbidity or something rotten
When all I mean is the exhilarating past –
Two laps of a grass or cinder track in under
Two minutes and the pathos of a grown man
Condemned to find his consolation in small wins
Remembered while holding his old running shoes,
As if I've grown old, comic, and vulnerable.
Where did it go, my lungful body, my wholehearted
Momentum of self and sheer self-interest?
I didn't predict this ambitionlessness –
A will to survive without self-pity or -parody.
There are other wretchednesses, other defeats.
Is it honesty, or the simple meaning of art,

To touch on selflessness that's loathed when known,
Or only that there's nowhere left to go
Other than the place of the old and unthanked?

Venezuela

Your poetry sounded like spoken salsa.
I am in love with your language, courtesies,
Hospitality, the way you spoke to me.
I could write like this for a very long time
And I could even write like this in rhyme.
Through the traffic of Caracas, I overheard
The song of the improbable linnet,
And the sorrows of Bolívar, of whom
I'm far from fit to speak – a man my size,
With a dead love, but a real hero.

'O brave new world that has such noises in it!'

I could wear a brimmed hat and smoke cigars
On a verandah in my coffee plantation
(If I had one) holding up my rum punch
To catch the sunset in its tawny depths.

I could do that. I could do lots of things.
But probably, I'll do nothing at all.
There's something in me that insists it sings
Freely, for nothing, the lovely, lonely art
Called poetry, an art you understand.

The Wasp House

We used to listen to its papery hum –
Entrances, exits, the constant to-and-from
Inhuman industry of it.
Spun from its citizens' juices, it was home,
Factory and cellular prison
Designed and built in one athletic night,
Or so it seemed to us discovering it
In the viburnum.

I had to have my daily peek. Spilled wasps
Covered their colony, dripping like syrups
All over it. Fierce, relentless, they brought
A hazard to our gardened nature.
Singular instinct seethed from the wasp house.
Their traffic was all obsession,
Imperial, devoted to frantic
Commerce and necessity.

An empty city swaying in the wind
Marked winter and it was like watching
A civilization diminish and fall.
Air-archaeology is what we work with,
Sifting through what isn't there
As if their secret's one we have to find,
A loss that feels like a non-event,
A life as weightless as their wings.

East Riding

'You wouldn't recognize the place. It's changed.'
For me, though, it can never cease to be
Outlandish shadows, all it was, distilled
Into five minutes' worth of memory,
A summary of years, unsought, unwilled,
Arising from unasked-for loping light
In which my mind is disarranged
And harks back to a non-specific night
Dated for 1969, and there –
A held hand, fragrance, leaves, a kiss, and air.

It's navigation by internal stars
On visits such as these into the past
Country, in which the dead must reappear
Beside me, holding on, and holding fast,
Reluctant to be there, but ah! so dear.
The leaf-trapped stars are all in place before
Agog in-love astronomers
Who enter through a land's botanic door
Into themselves, with all of Holderness
Surrounding them, and part of their caress.

Some landscapes never change, because they stay
Unvisited as too significant
For a return, and must remain the same.
A stern but loved voice warns me off with 'Don't!'
And I obey it, drawing back from shame
To tell myself, 'No, don't ever go back.
Just let it always be the way
It was' – life-beaten, off the beaten track –

'The house in Ryehill that we almost bought,
And stars that in the starlit trees were caught.'

What happens happens as it has to do
And an intelligence can try, but can't
Succeed in finding out all reasons why
That, this, or that occurred. Recalcitrant,
All life can make is its domestic cry
Into eternal silence's untoward
Realm of the intimate and true,
The very meaningful and the absurd –
Patrington's pub player-piano, and tea
Taken in Hedon or in Withernsea.

Bête Noire's Edition of *Terry Street*
with Photographs by Robert Whitaker

Memory dims nothing, not even a tyro's delusions;
But it probes with questions – 'How could you neglect
Pickled onions, the untroubled children's smiles,
Flowers in pails, hairnets, Kirby grips, and discarded prams?'

'Great was thy love for something or other,' a voice says
From a shadow, a wry, ironic and affectionate voice.
Better to have printed young feeling than avoided it.
Better by far a self's honesty and its ordinary days.

Such, though, are memory's pleasures and sorrows
Delivered in late-night silence under a standard lamp
When listening to the rustles of night, trees, and a river,
Reminiscing to the tempos of domestic splendour.

Martyn Chalk's photographed olive-green mini-van means
Martyn and Dee are sitting in our two-roomed house
With Lesley and me, while the dauntless Bob Whitaker
Goes about taking his gifted and truthful photographs.

Thirty-one years ago on a day of early summer!
Love, life, death, love, and children, since 1968
Add up to enormous subtractions and additions
Examined by old street-women watching at curtains

As if I am always to be held under their scrutiny.
Matriarchal raised eyebrows and quizzical censure,
Old men's ancestral surmises and extinct stares –
They're preserved for ever in photographs and a few words.

We were sitting on squeaky bamboo furniture, anxious
For the preservation of Bob Whitaker's 'Triumph',

[69]

His girlfriend in Antipodean shorts and long socks
Among the Dusty Springfields and Julie Christies,

Beehives, rollers, maternity wear and mini-skirts
And their men of hard work, motorbikes and small pay.
We saw them that evening in Martyn and Dee's house.
They came through the door with the éclat of Sixties
    superstars.

It was a very good day of 1968, and – God help me –
I was to be published in the *London Magazine*, with
    photographs!
And one day I'd publish a book with my name on it!
I was so excited I was totally diffident. My *sang froid* was
    frozen.

I travel by bus, taxi, or train or plane, and reputation,
Which poets don't have anyway except among themselves
And a few others, leaves me at a dead loss for words.
Such is my street-inheritance, my non-driver's status.

Roll over, Larkin! 'Let me tell you the news …
Deliver me from days of old' … This is my mythology,
My witness that life is the best thing that can happen to us,
That it is warm with laughter, love, complaints, and tragedies.

I can feel and see these two rooms very clearly
Down to the last details of their decoration – blue Tintawn,
Table, chairs, curtains, books and typewriter, a music stand,
A sketch pad on a cushion in the windowed sun.

Back, too, comes my obsessive concern with the outside lav's
Draughts and exposures or, after running, a stand-up wash
In the narrow and diminutive so-called kitchen, or in –
Lawrentian, *truly* working-class! – a tin bath in the
    living-room.

Good to have walked behind a hand-plough with horses
As a boy, pestering the ploughman, and to have bathed
In a tin bath in the living-room. Good, too, to have known
How hard the past was, while being privileged in it.

It's as if I'm just that little bit older than I really am.
And then I think of the clouds that have passed, days and
    nights,
Thousands of watch-windings, and that poetry is
Consolations of shame and averted perfections.

Other things, too, it might be, or demand – devotion,
Surrender to impulses only half-understood in their time,
Giving in hopelessly to self's grammar, to selfishness,
In the hope of art, and of something not unfinished.

Outsider, incomer, not on first-name terms with my
    neighbours,
The hardest understanding, I know, is never to have
    understood
Entirely those among whom I lived, and who did not,
    entirely,
Understand me, as if a true exchange were not permitted.

Whatever the anthropology of that two-year occasion,
I worry still that reform should be seen as a threat
And not as a kiss, that the idealism of Then feels
Identical to that of Now, and that nothing's been changed.

I speak with a full heart, conscious of believing in what is
    best,
Whether neighbours, flowers, books, beer, or pickled onions,
Aware, too, that the revolutionary momentum within me
Survives as the same idealism, an indestructible cry

Persevering despite whatever happens, in love with
Moonlit rivers, my children, the whole wide world,
And if all this is close to the unbearably intimate
Then allow me, at least, to call it my poem, dedicated to –

Not to the dead (enough of that) – but to Bob Whitaker,
Who came back from the dead, who was the Beatles'
    photographer,
Who helped me preserve what I knew, who added his
    optical art
To my love, my life, and to the times we have lived through,

And to my neighbours of then, whom I hardly knew,
Who knew little of me or us except through what they
    saw ...
An interruption to grammar – the poem I'm trying to write
Means memory, means love, means two melodic rooms.

Martagon Lilies

Here, then, is the painting, a sought-after
Botanical icon to commemorate her
Colourist philosophy. I'll weave around it
Invisible webs of pleasure, life and wit,
A vase, a table, a cool room in a *bastide*
South of somewhere Martagon lilies grow
In shade, a purple archipelago,
A wave of wonder in a world of weed.

Or white, as in *Lilium martagon album*,
Waxy and creamy, the least cumbersome
Plant in the world next to the Old Turk's Cap.
To chart its nature means scanning the map
Of Europe and Asia, from Portugal, east
Into Siberia and the Yenisei
Tracked down by an intrepid botanist
In sturdy boots, beneath a Turkish sky,

An eastern European sky, Mongolian sky,
Or in the Caucasus, sent out to ply
The tenderest trade, the study of the lily.
Only too willingly, too readily,
Would I give myself to that science of beauty.
I dream that one day I might come across
Martagons growing in a glade. Duty
Forbids such dreams, but I dream, and my loss

Becomes what Peter calls 'a piece of real'.
In my tweeded and booted dream, I feel
My way into a forest, and, in a clearing,
Discover martagons, my botaneering

Dream true in dream. Relative poverty
Prevents such wanted expeditions to
Far-off places. I keep my liberty
To dream myself into 'a piece of true'.

These are strange lilies. They survive for years
In wooded sunlessness, and then appear
When trees collapse, and light gets through to their
Bulb, rhizome or stolon foodstore, and air,
Sunlight, enough to stir them, makes them alive
Enough to thrust a spike of purple glory
Into oaked heat, shouting 'We can survive,
And darkness is only part of our story!'

Peploe knew flowers, and fruits. He knew them well.
Hats, drawing-rooms and ladies were Cadell,
Pure sailor-fixated, while Fergusson
Went in for the voluptuous, hard-on
After hard-on, full of the warm South
As only a north-man can be, café scenes,
Picnic scenes, curvaceous nudes, the wet mouth
Of his paint, and his erotic leans

Into a picture. And the best you bought
For the Ferens! Leslie Hunter's houseboat
And flowers fitted in nicely with your
Art-lover's precious optical amours.
You were so positive! I feel ashamed
Even after all those years of living with
Your taste in painting, and my own tastes maimed
By memory. Are you legend, are you myth

To me, that you should exert such a close
Posthumous hold over me? I suppose
It's all my fault. And Peploe's picture sheds

No light on darker truths. His lily-heads
Seem poised before abstraction. They'll fade soon –
The browning leaf, the blue, the white, the black,
Are all unplaceable. Is it afternoon
Indoors or out, or where? By what playback

Can I enter his eye? Is it a napkin,
Or folds of aesthetic white that draw me in?
What's that greeny black, that black, and pink,
That blue, that white? I look, and blink, and think
Beauty, not meaning, 's what I see, a pure
Picture of lilies in an anywhere.
I think, and think again, then I'm unsure
If what I breathe is art- or lily-air.

I browse the Caucasus. Oak-beech pastures
Of fern, in high country, yield my pleasures,
Discoveries of martagons. In chestnut forests,
I join the ranks of probing botanists.
The insufficiency of dreams leaves me
Fraudulent, a lily-lover but lily-fraud
In expertise, though growing them un-grieves me
With handfork-chink, weed pull, and hoe-prod.

Were I less literary, I might live
With form and colour, without narrative.
Instead, I argue. I can say a meadow,
Woodland, roses, and the colour of snow,
But not leave them alone. So, I adore
Peploe's de-vocalized melodiousness
And his infatuated eye, the *more, more,
More* of it, his vision's sheer harmlessness.

I've searched in it for meaning, but found none.
As for story, or moral – there isn't one.

I believe in the wild, and botany,
Forms, colours, scents, no whiff of irony
In perfect, perfumed woodland, in the leaf,
Flower, herb, meadow, and floral grasslands
Stretching towards infinity's *as if*,
In being kind, in the holding of hands.

Early Hours in Dairsie

2 follows 1, etcetera, night dusk,
Day dawn, and so we go, as Shakespeare says,
As syllables, a mere mumble of time.

A ghostly heron rises in the mist.
Three, four, five flaps, and then it vanishes
Into its own shroud-coloured featheriness.

Cool-clearing mist drifts on the sleepless stream
Then a high slit of July blue appears.
'Why are you here?' says the chattering water.

'Why are you here?' says the dawn chorus.
'You aren't walking a dog, or heading for work
In the fields, so why are you here at this

Time by the Moonzie Burn at 5 a.m.?'
Do I need to explain, that I have come to see you,
And hear you? For you are beautiful,

And the weeds of water give off a cool scent
In these early hours, a fragrance of promises
Perfected by emergent, low sun.

I walked out to taste the freshness of summer.
Is that so suspicious? I like this bridge.
I am so very fond of you, this little strath,

With its burn, its high woodland to the west,
And far dew beginning to rise like smoke.
Who could refuse to get up from bed to walk

Among the cultivated peace of peace
Itself? I wouldn't call a country 'mine'.
But you *are* my country. You are birdsung;

You can do without my clumsy, human verse,
I know. Such sweetly chirruped cadences
Beat poetry into a cocked hat, but

I have to try at least to visit you
When you are at your best, in the cool dawn
Blending its moistures, sky showing through,

And should you find it smacks of loneliness,
I claim it's otherwise, and call it love,
My local and my universal kiss.

Indolence

The pleasure's one of its anticipation,
Knowing what will happen, when, where, though why –
For all my pondering – rarely gets answered.
It's the pleasure of expectedness,
Of the light breeze, birdsong, well-gardened air,
And vapour zips in the timetabled sky.

It's quite unexceptional, perfect peace
In a domesticity of one, civilian
To the point of irenic stasis, slothful
To a fault. An industrious bee wings past
Towards its buzzing labours. Blackbirds hop
From worm to worm. I stretch my idleness

And drop the book I tried but failed to read.
A hedgehog waddles down the weeded path.
A chaffinch, perched on a propped rake, chirps,
Then vanishes within my blink.
I have a bird in one eye and a trout
For my supper. I'm talking to myself

In my garden of indolence where I grow
Lethargy, lilies, and sit breathing mint,
Rosemary, thyme, sage, thinking of how I'll cook
That fine fat fish I caught in a mad moment
Devoted to dexterity and doing.
The breeze riffles the dropped unreadable book.

Shall I have chips with it, or baby potatoes?
Salad? Green beans? Or asparagus spears?
At this rate I'll be mentally exhausted
Before it's time to cook and eat. Aha!

I could have deep-fried bad book ... Thank God
For chairs, cushions, blue sky, and peace and quiet.

I so much looked forward to my day off.
Now that it's here, what I looked forward to,
I realize, was doing damn all in a deckchair.
Thank God, too, for this Chablis, black olives,
Sunshine, and all these fragile butterflies,
Busy, beautiful, and living their lives

As if there's no tomorrow. Kick the book.
That's the stuff! Boot it away. I'll leave it
Out here on the grass. It won't improve it.
All this is *my* property! My goods and chattels,
Impedimenta, my but-and-ben, mine own
Estate and little home, and all for me ...

Another airliner – high energy,
Sky-power, propulsion, and momentum,
Exactly what I'm doing without today
By being bum-bound on a comfy chair.
Can't I get off my butt and *do something*?
Well, no – frankly. It's my day off, my first

In weeks. I've done enough. It's time to do
Nothing, for controlled irresponsibility.
I'm relaxing. The bird in my right eye
Fidgets. Sun does funny things to the leaves.
Hedgehog 's back! Is it a he or a she?
It goes past me like a self-propelled handbag.

I need to pee. But if I go inside
I'll be tempted to stay. Well, it's my grass,
And there's no one about ... So here goes water.
Deeply, I regret having pissed on the book.

Much worse, though, is I think I've doused a daisy
Which didn't deserve it. One day, I might invent

A board or card game, but for one player –
It won't be called 'Solitaire'. I'll call it
'Time on *My* Side', or else 'As *I* Like It'.
I'm lying low, but coming up for air.
My wandering mind patrols its boundaries.
There are some things I like better than this –

A walk along a beach on Bernaray,
Laughing with Lillias in the summer-house
I can't yet bring myself to call a 'gazebo'.
Or dozing in Vienna over coffee.
And other things, equally innocent ...
Some might be physical. Not one means 'work'.